The Worst

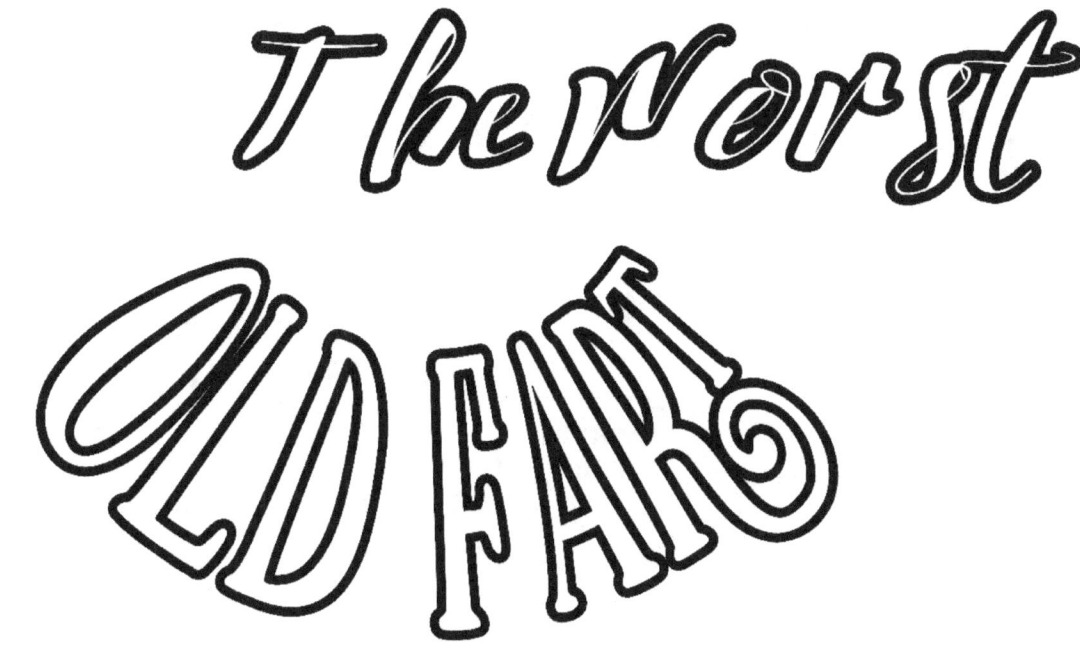

OLD FART

Phenomenal Swear Word To Color

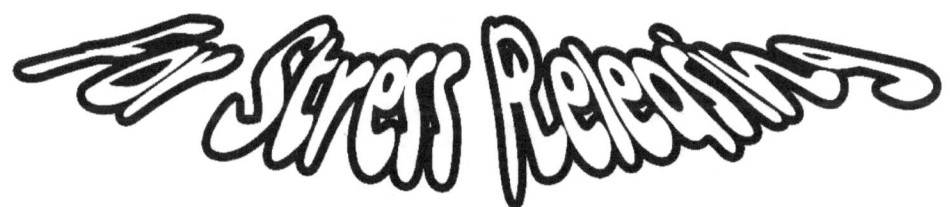

For Stress Releasing

C.J. Willoughby

Happy Coloring!

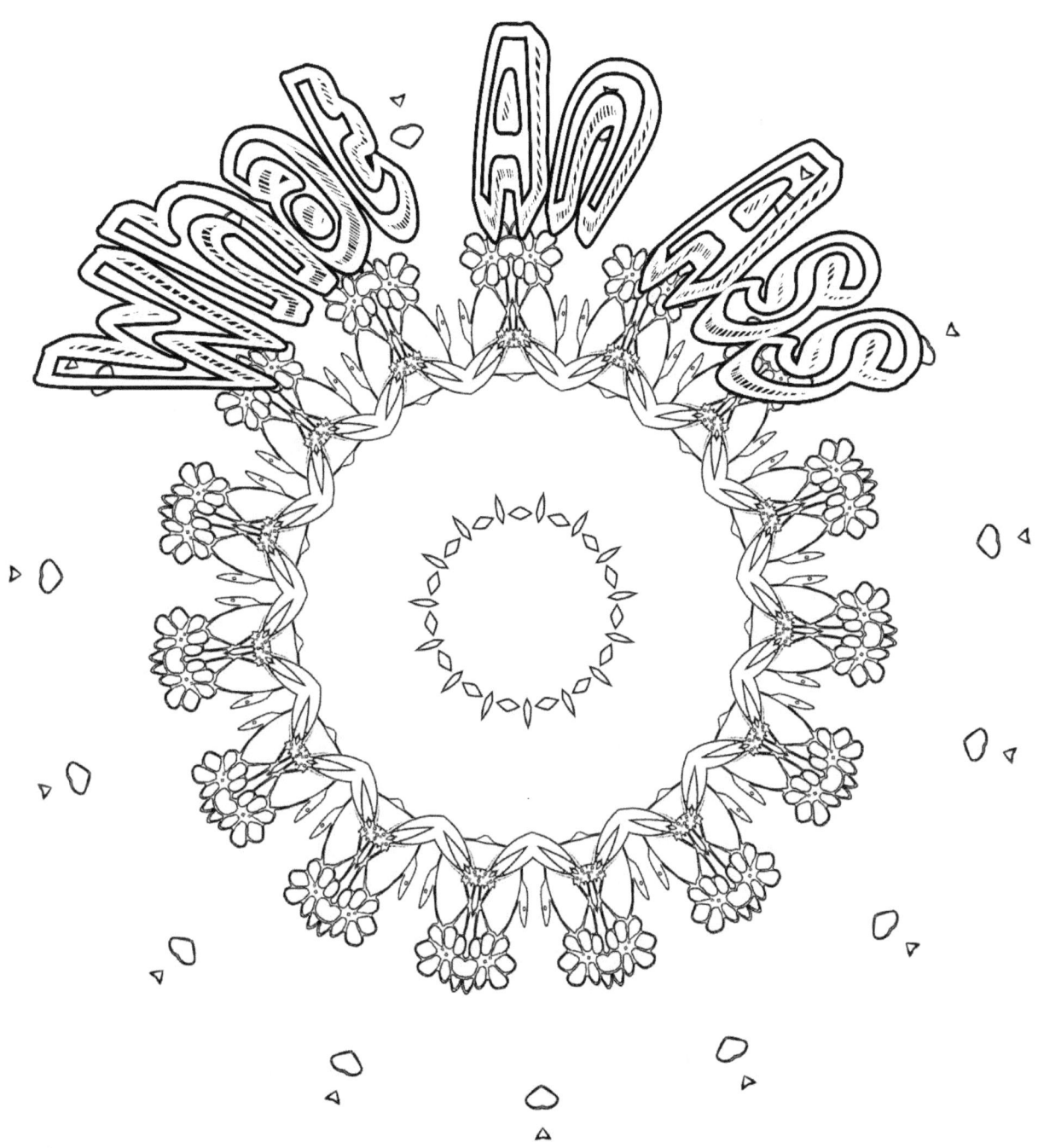

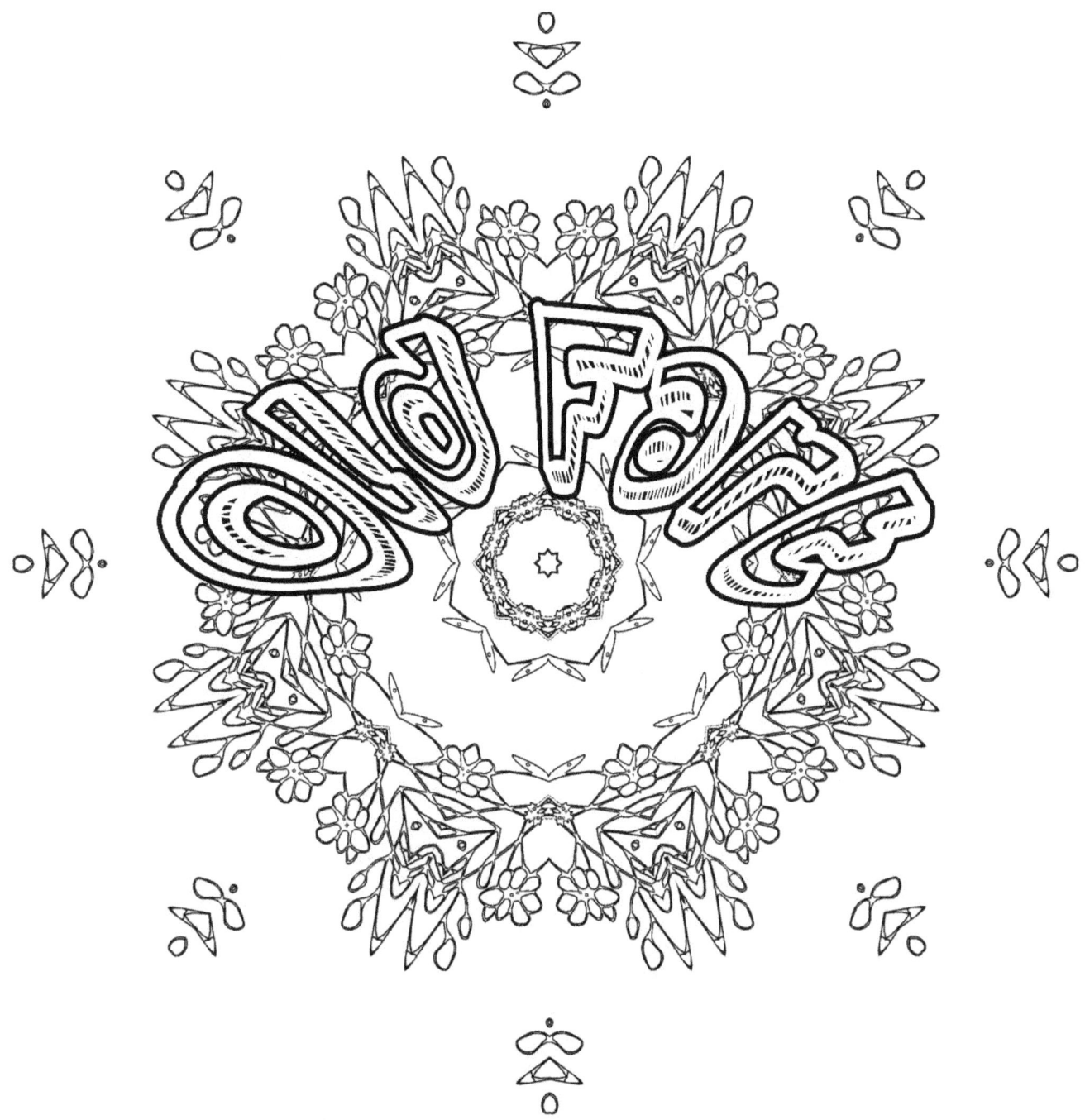

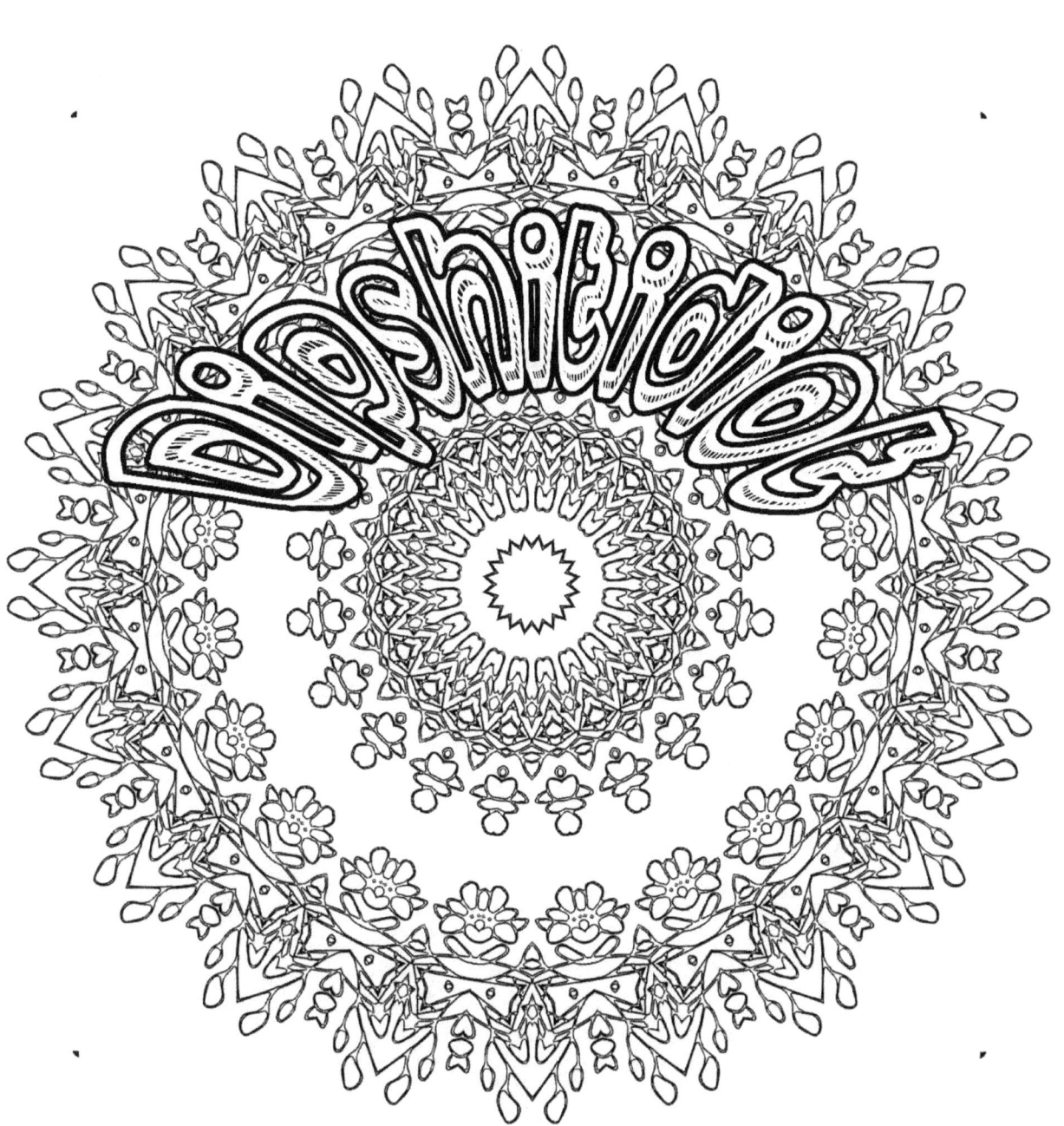

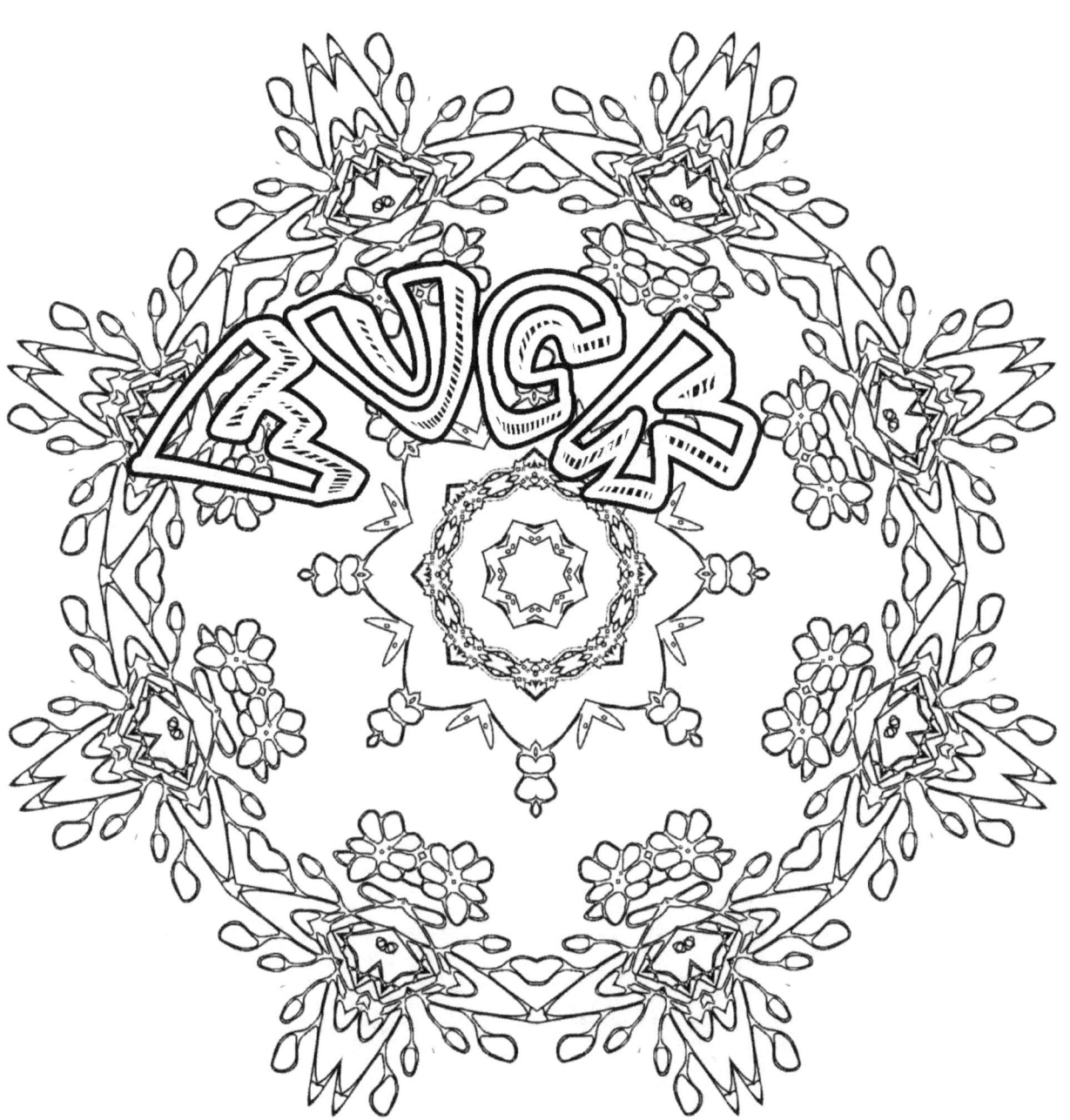

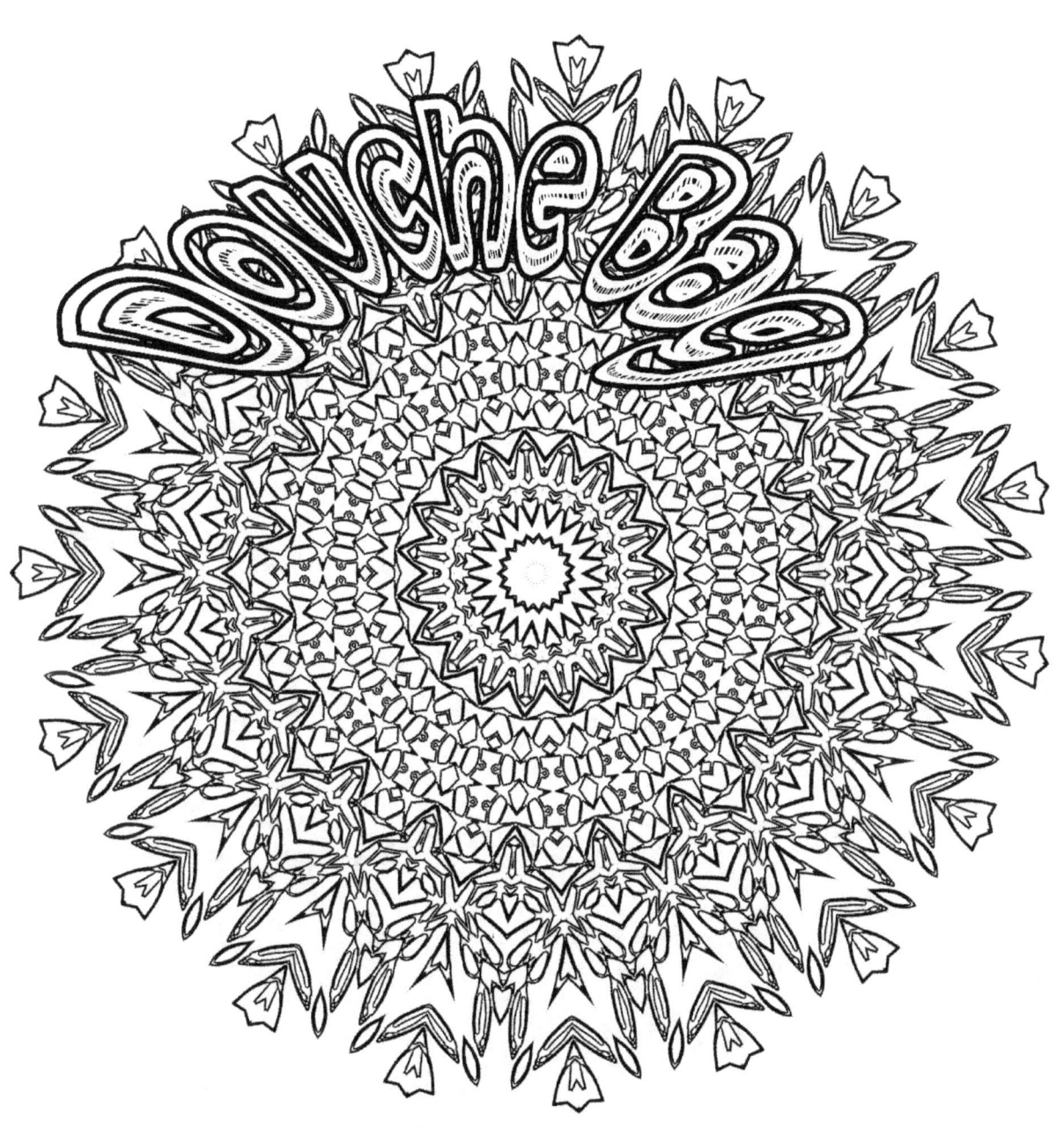

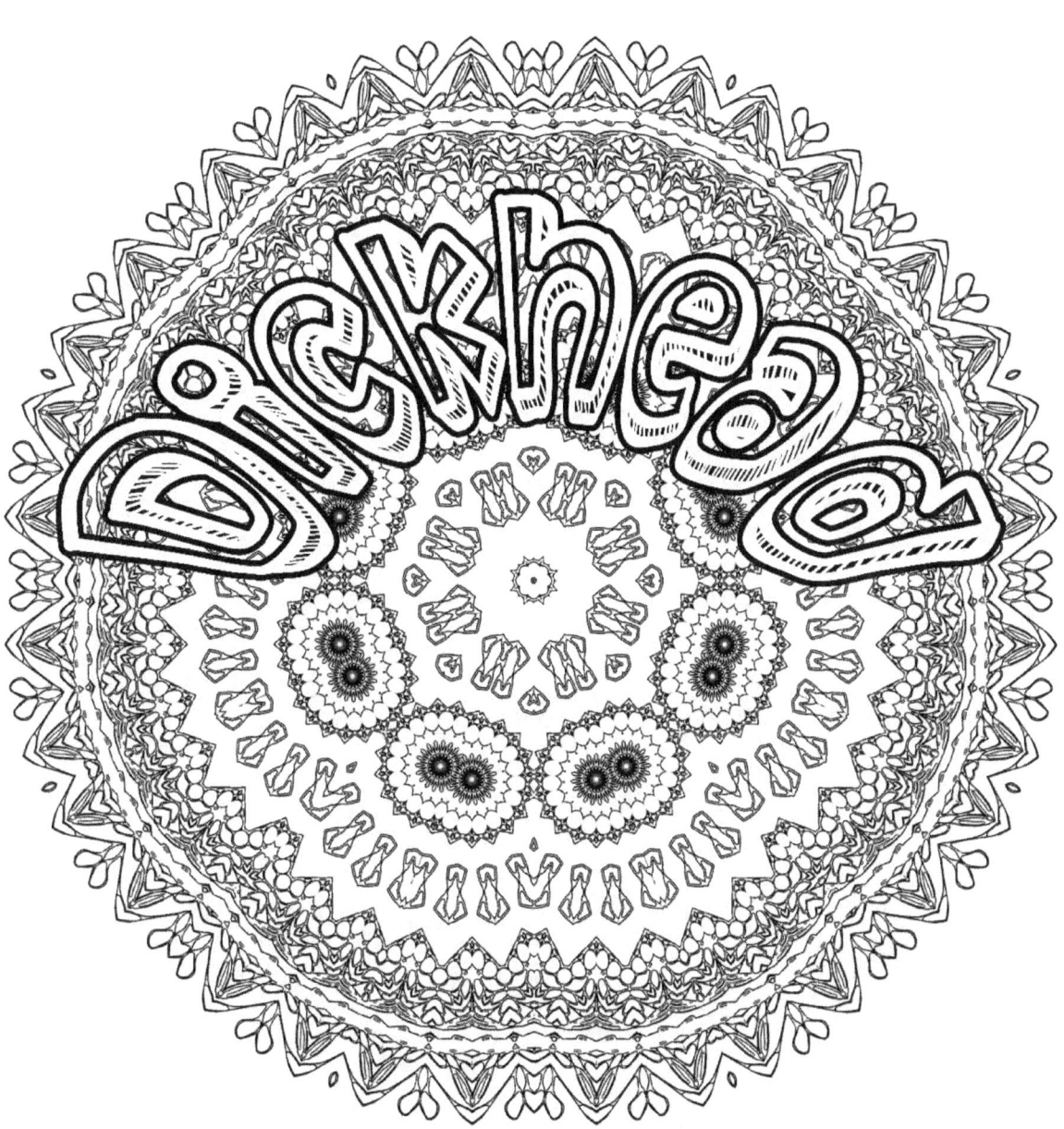

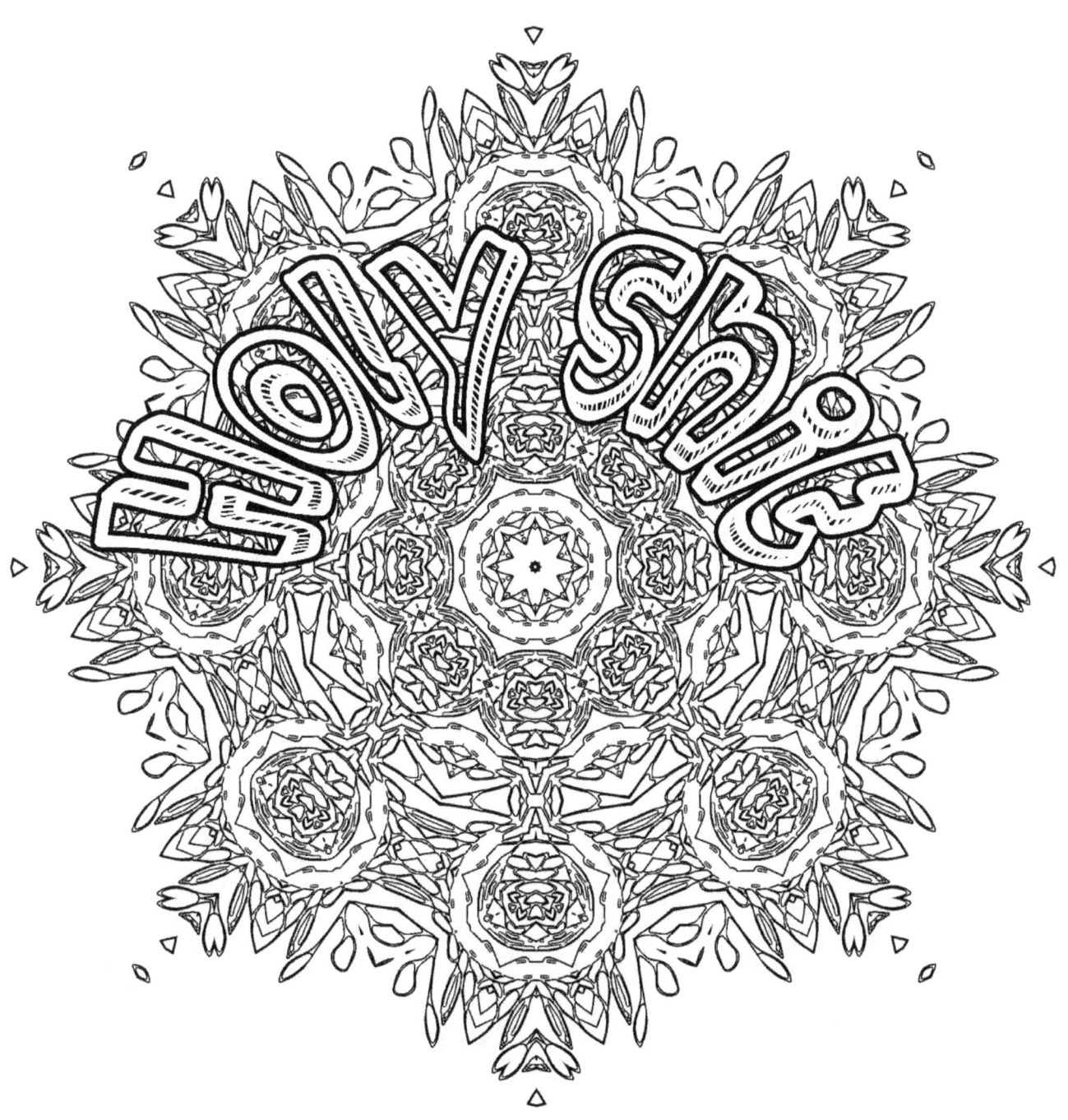

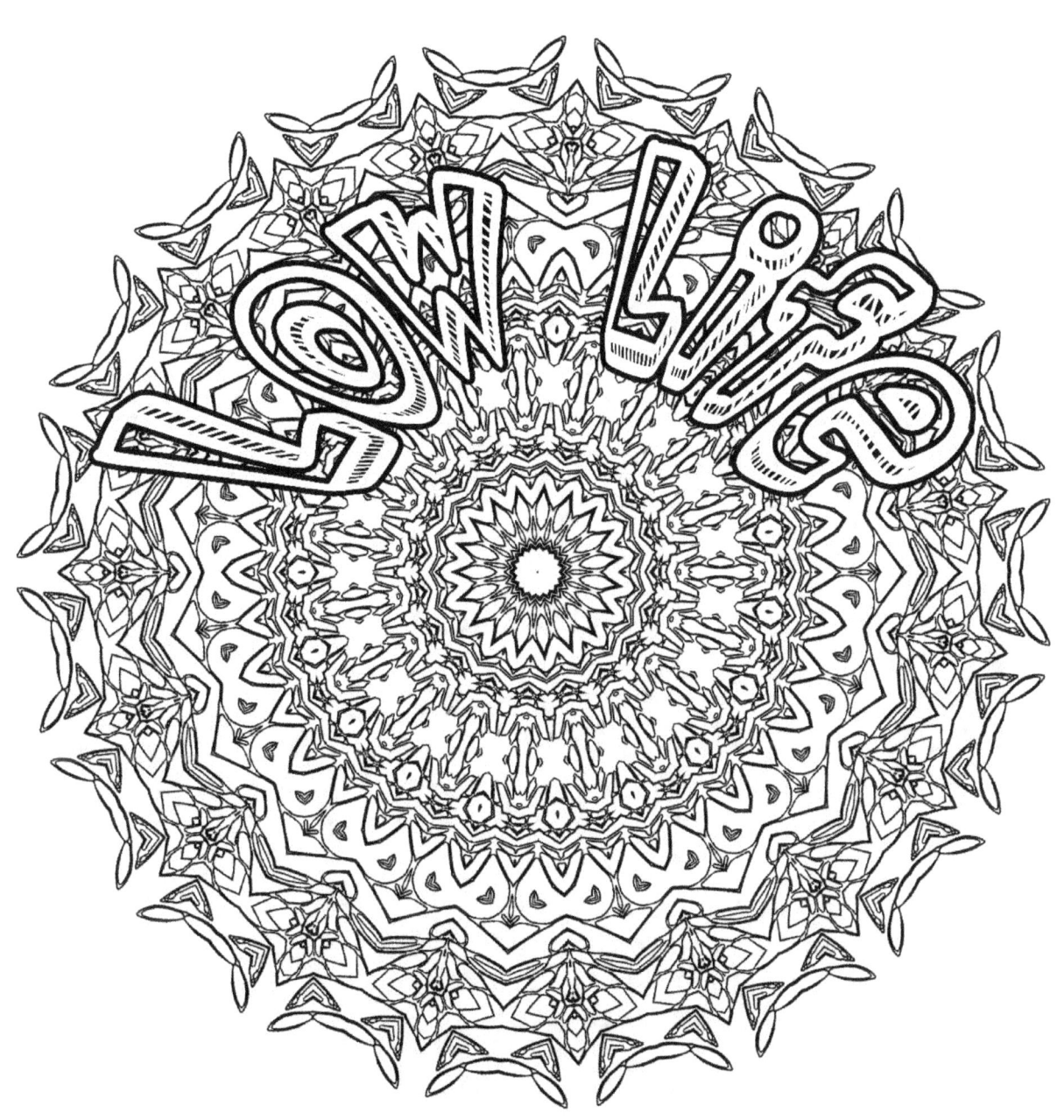

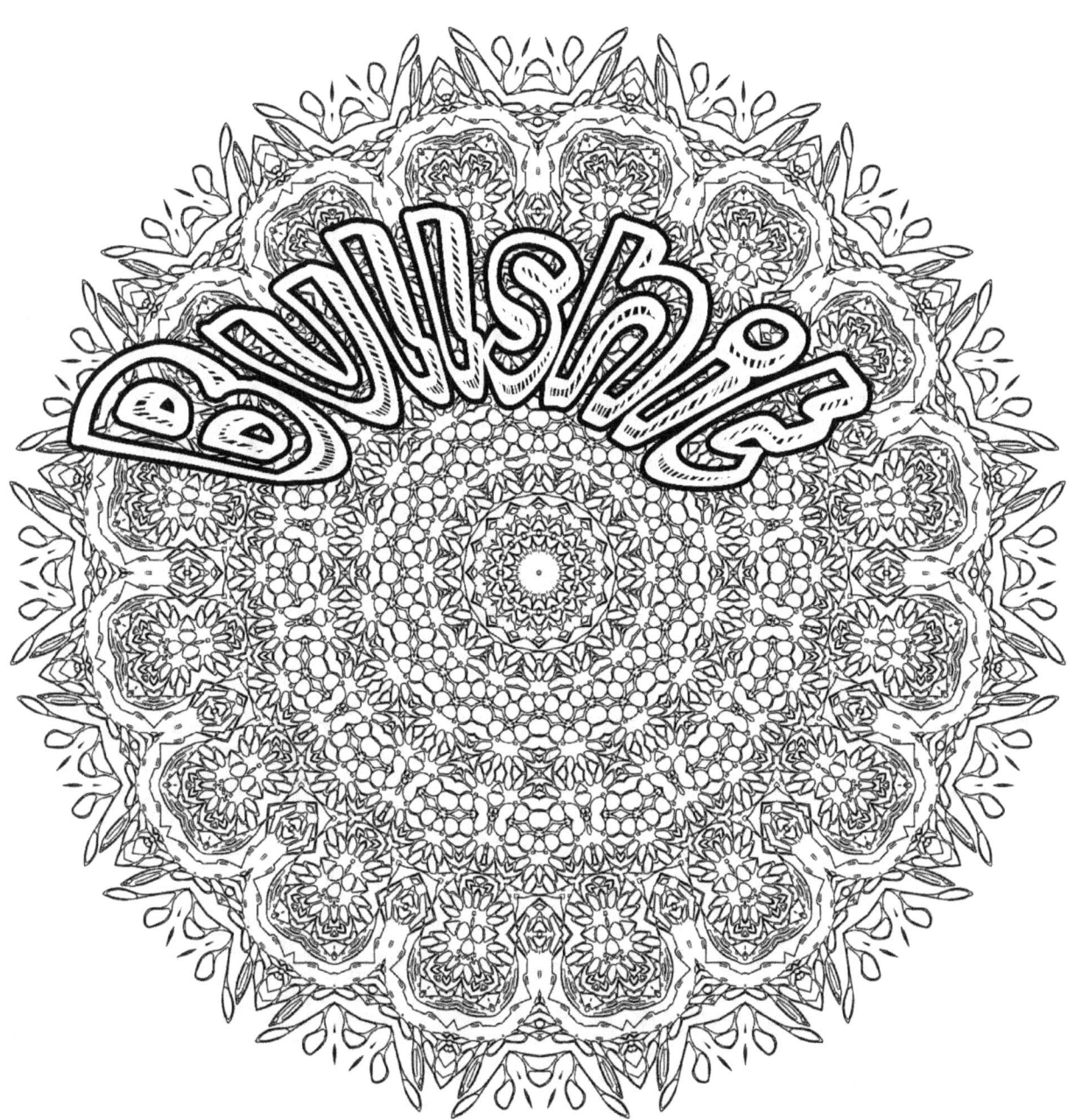

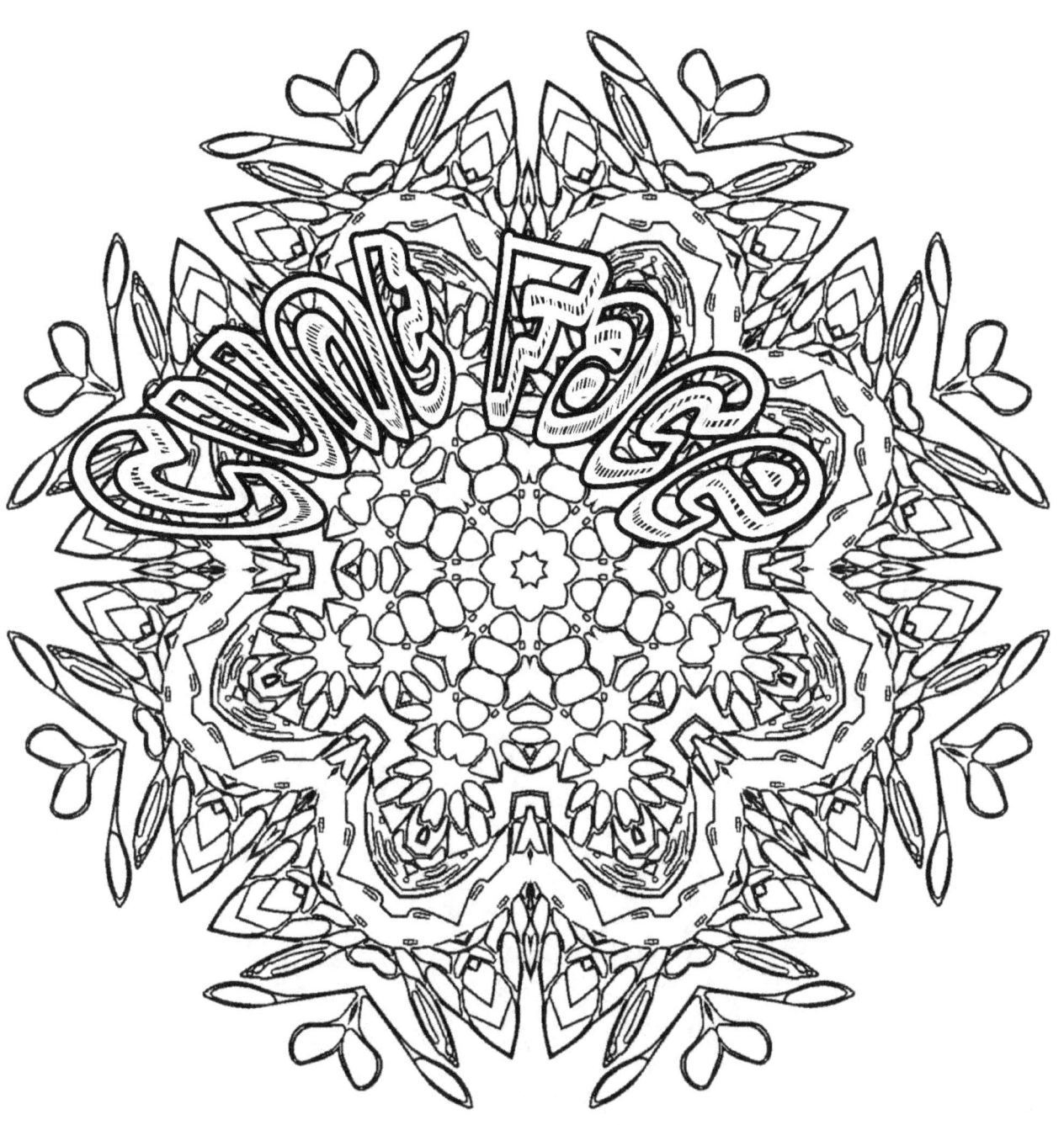

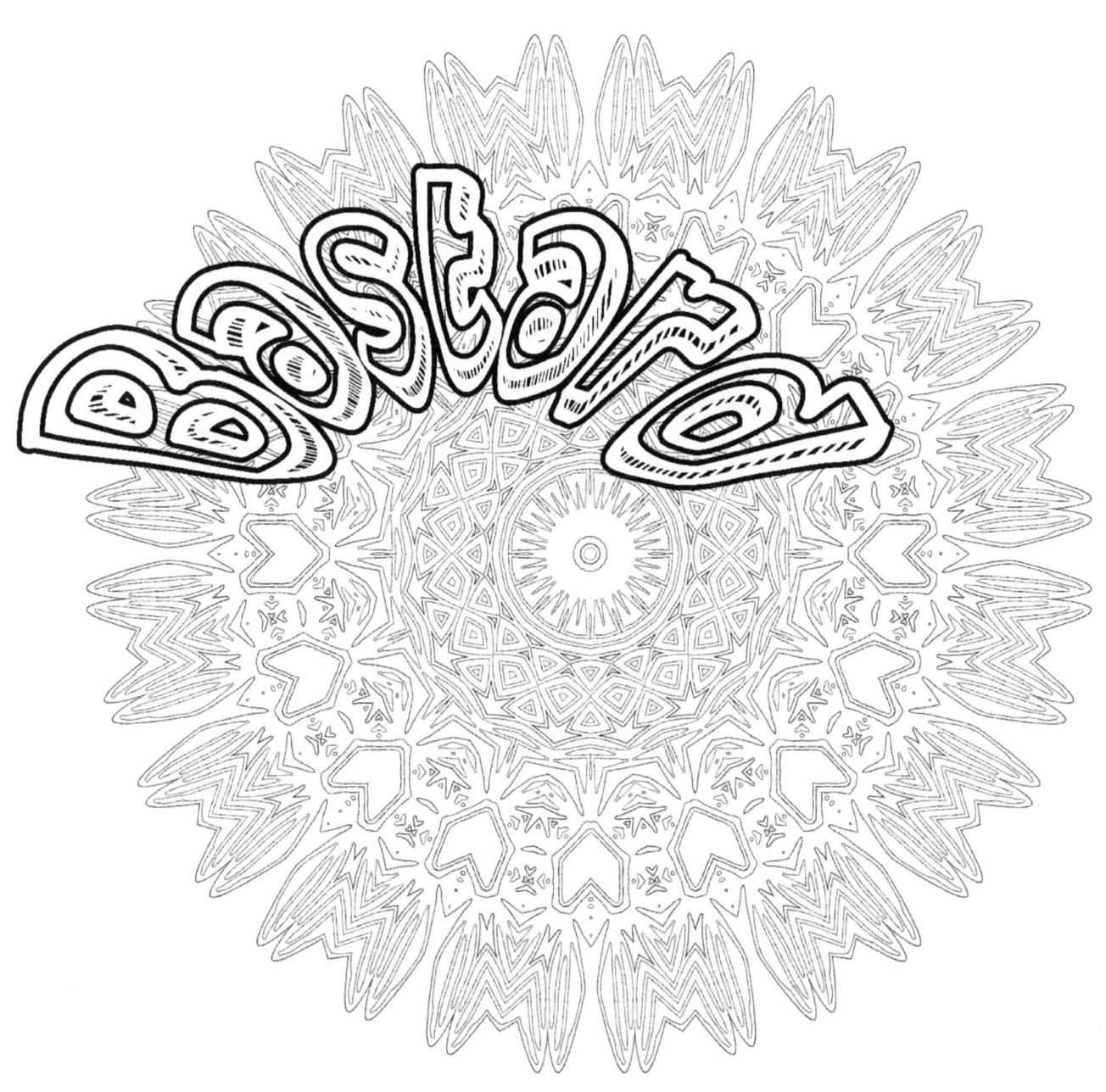

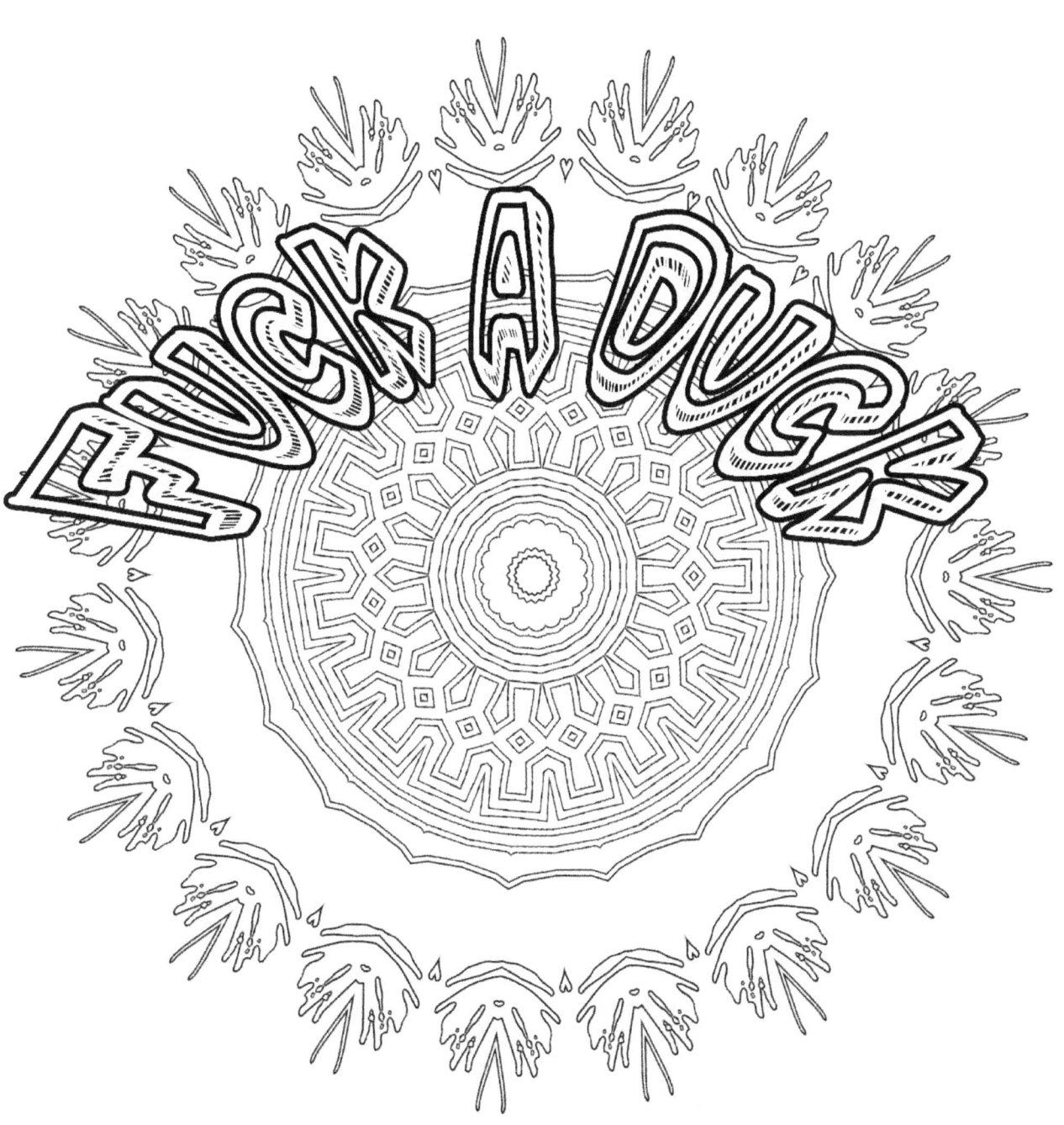

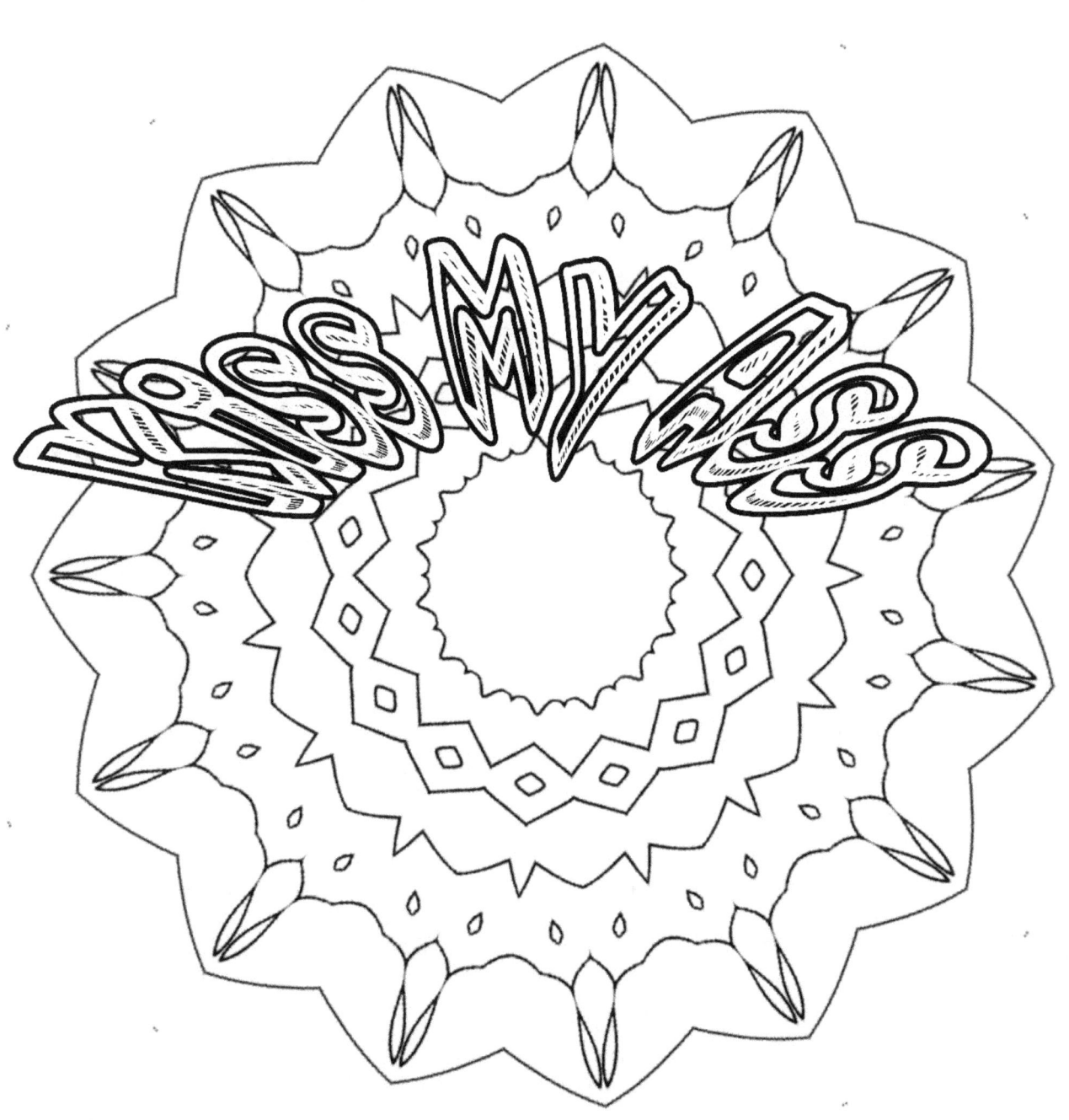

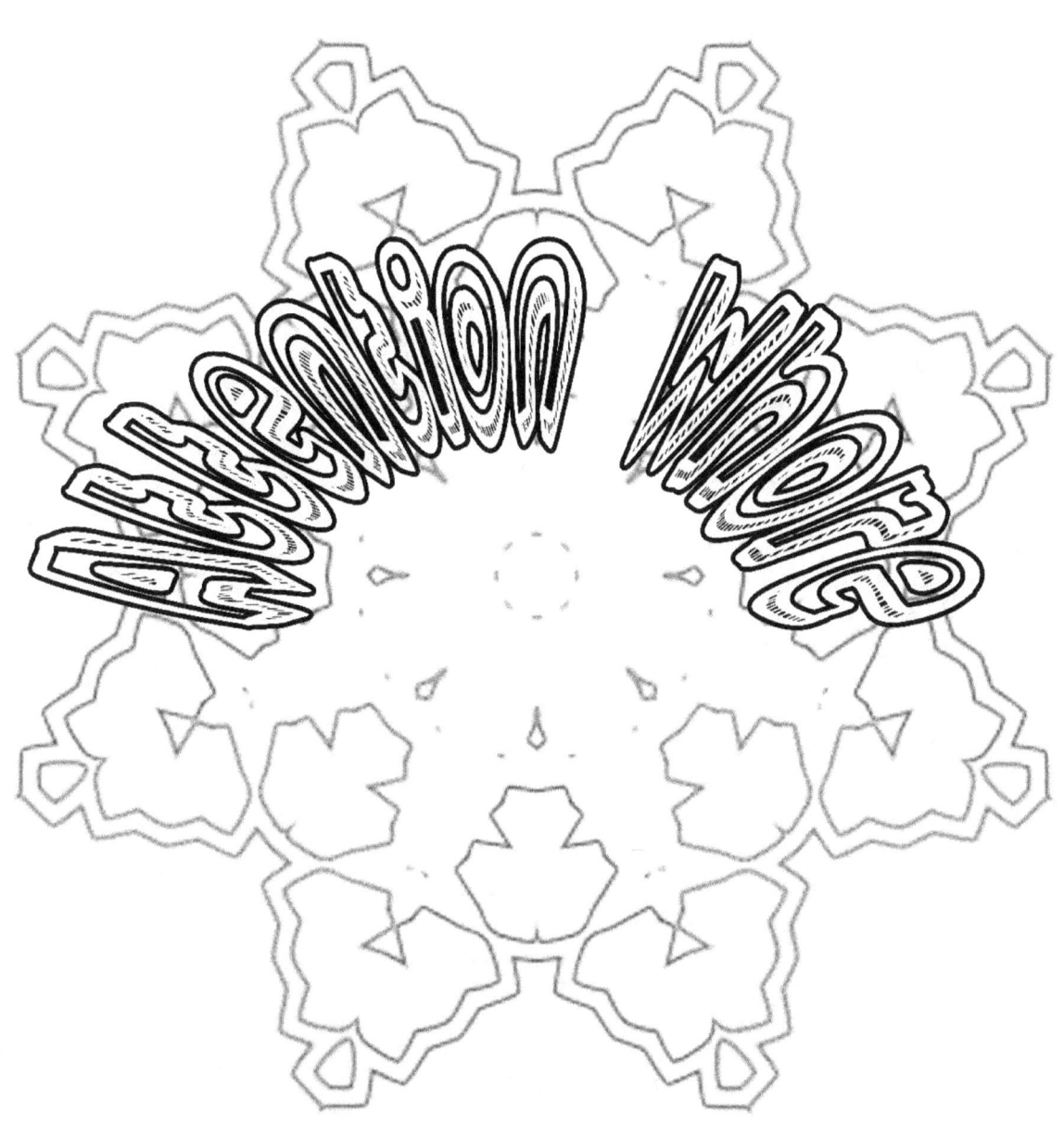

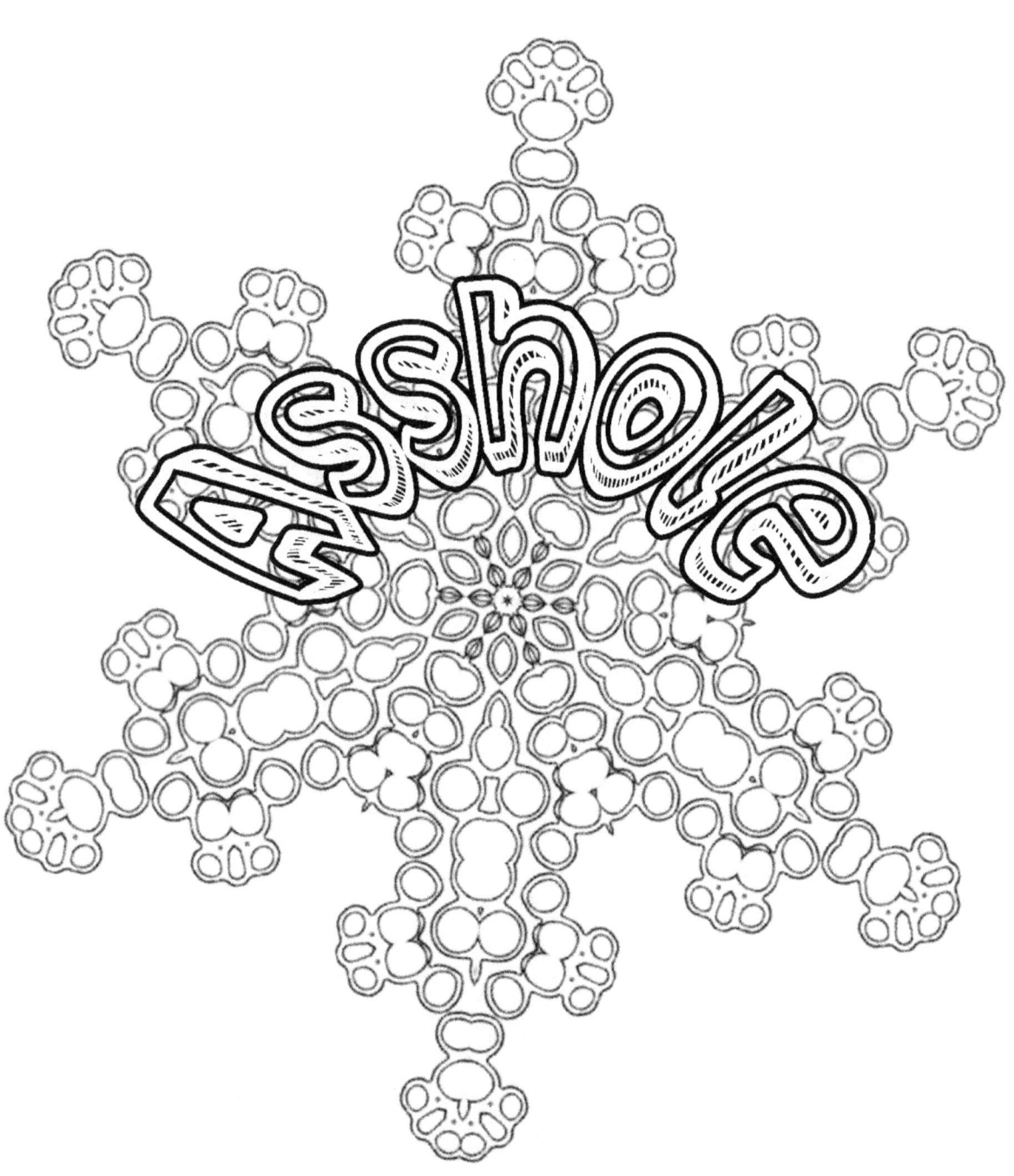

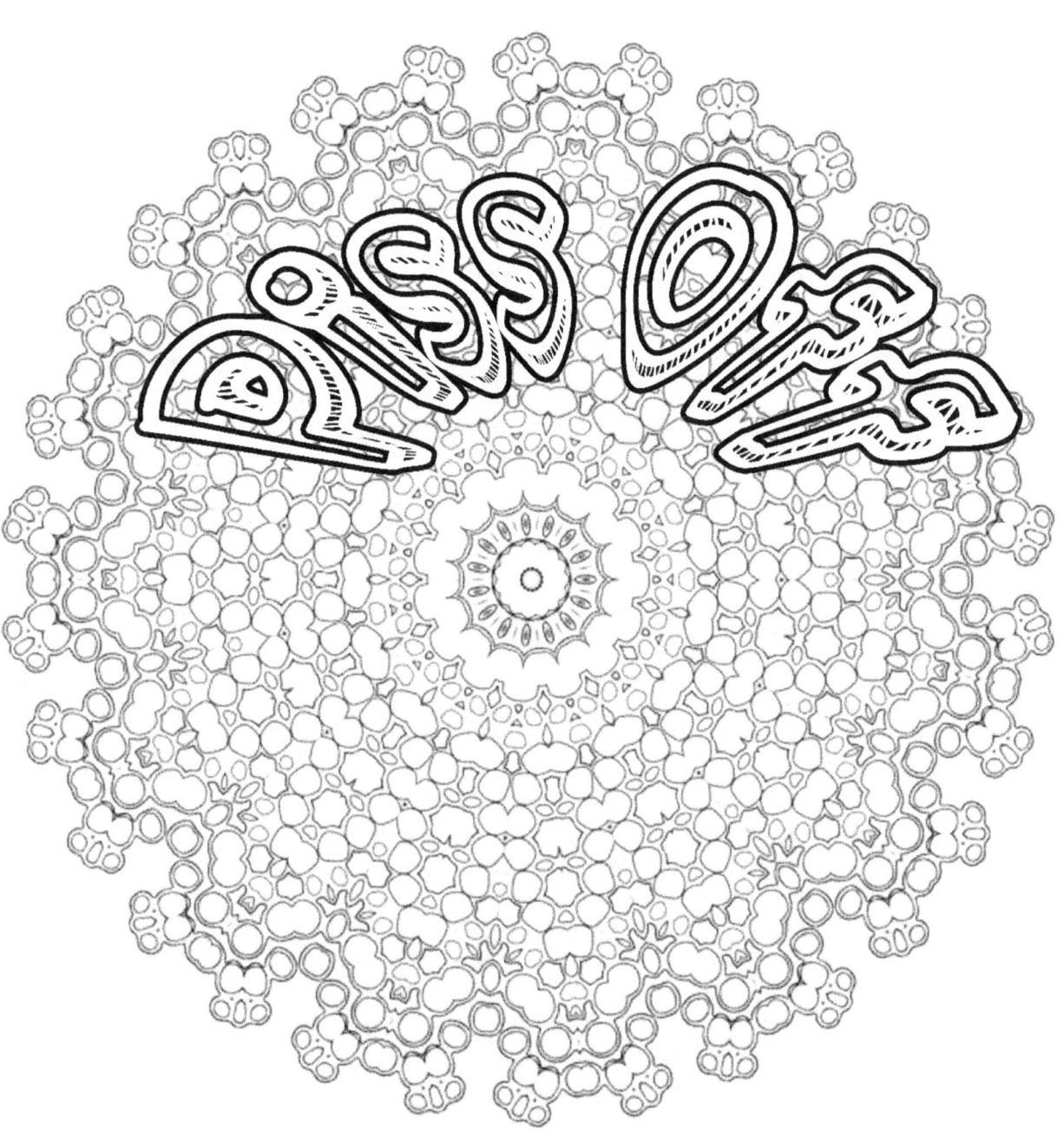

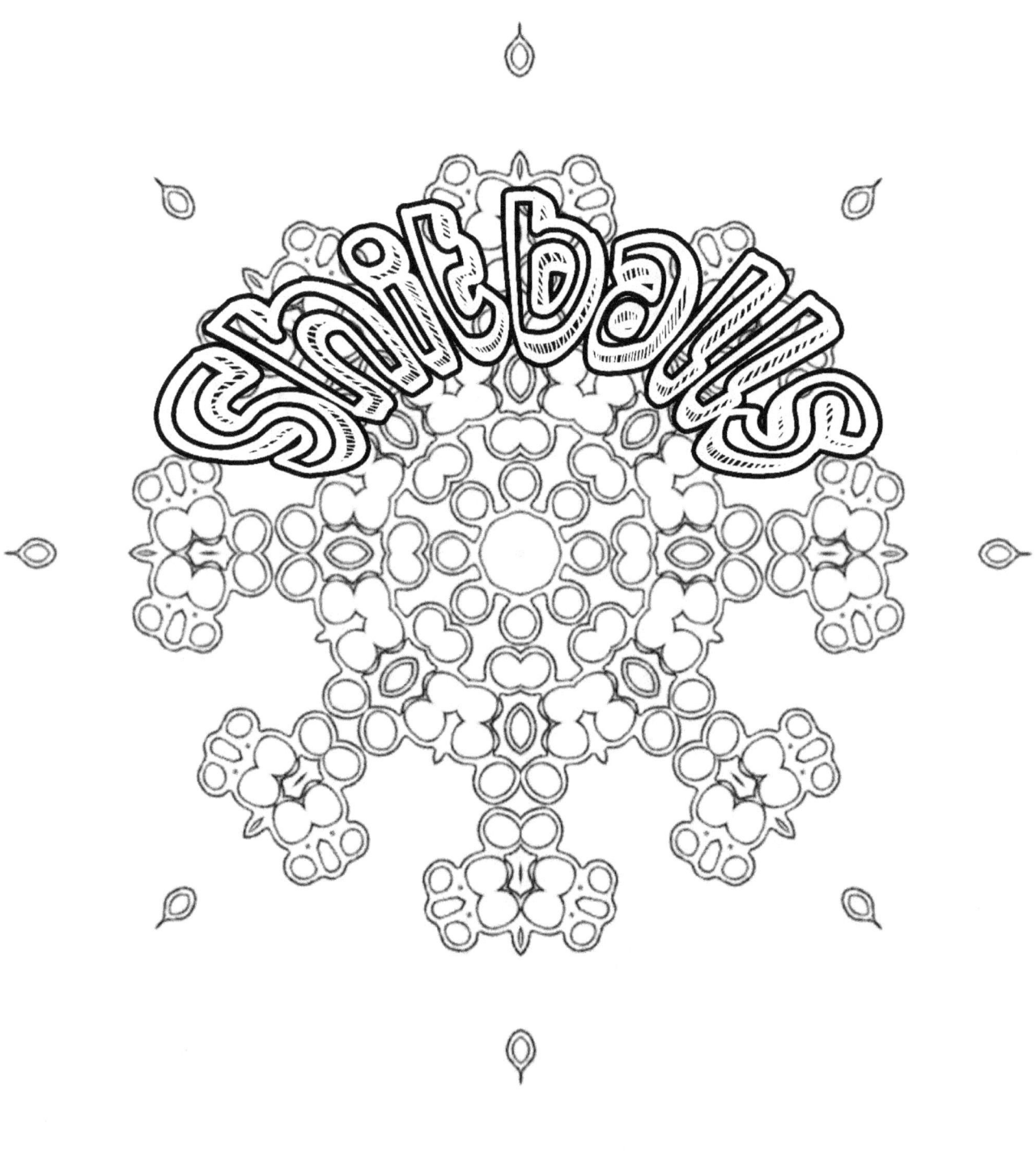

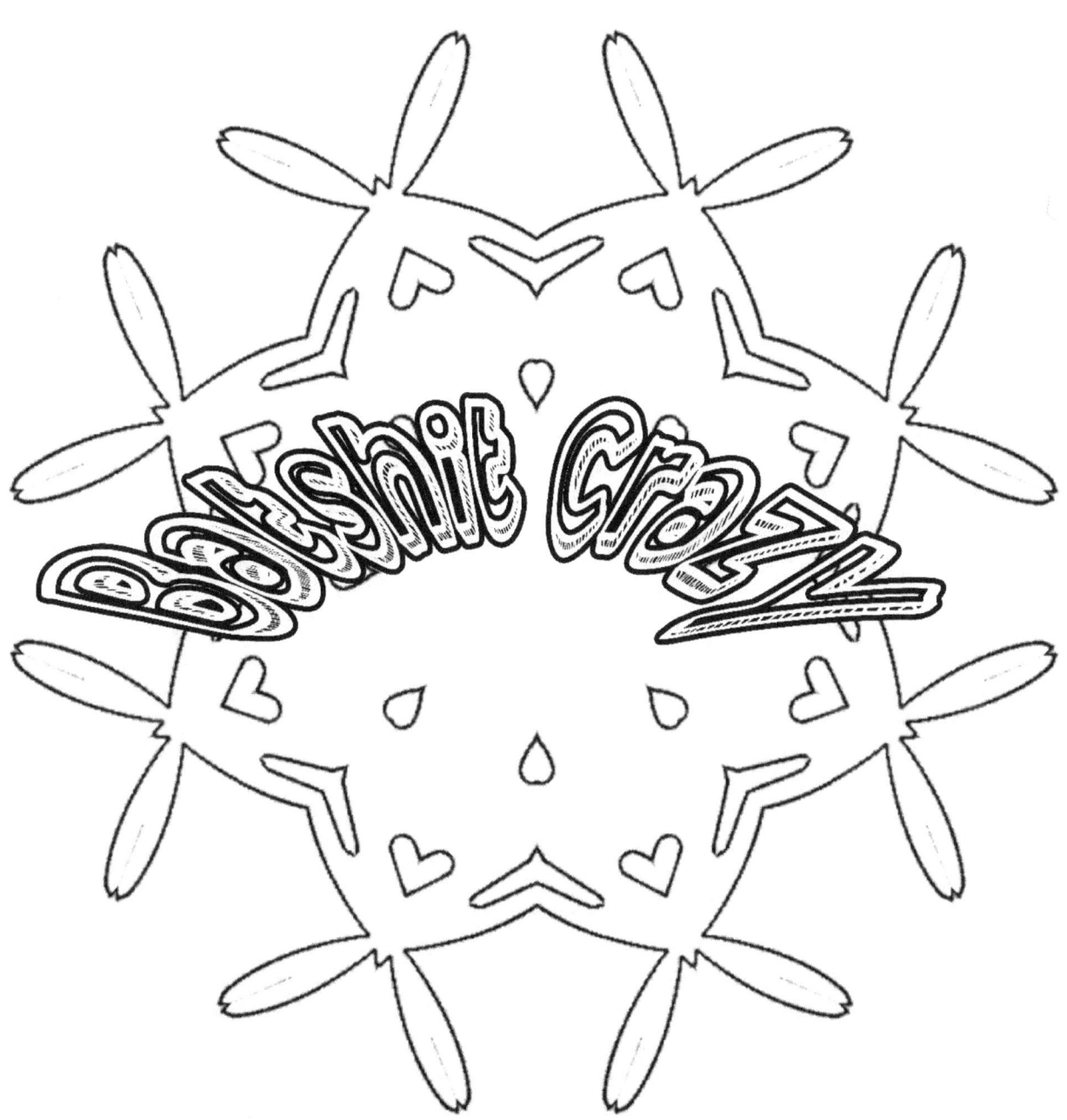

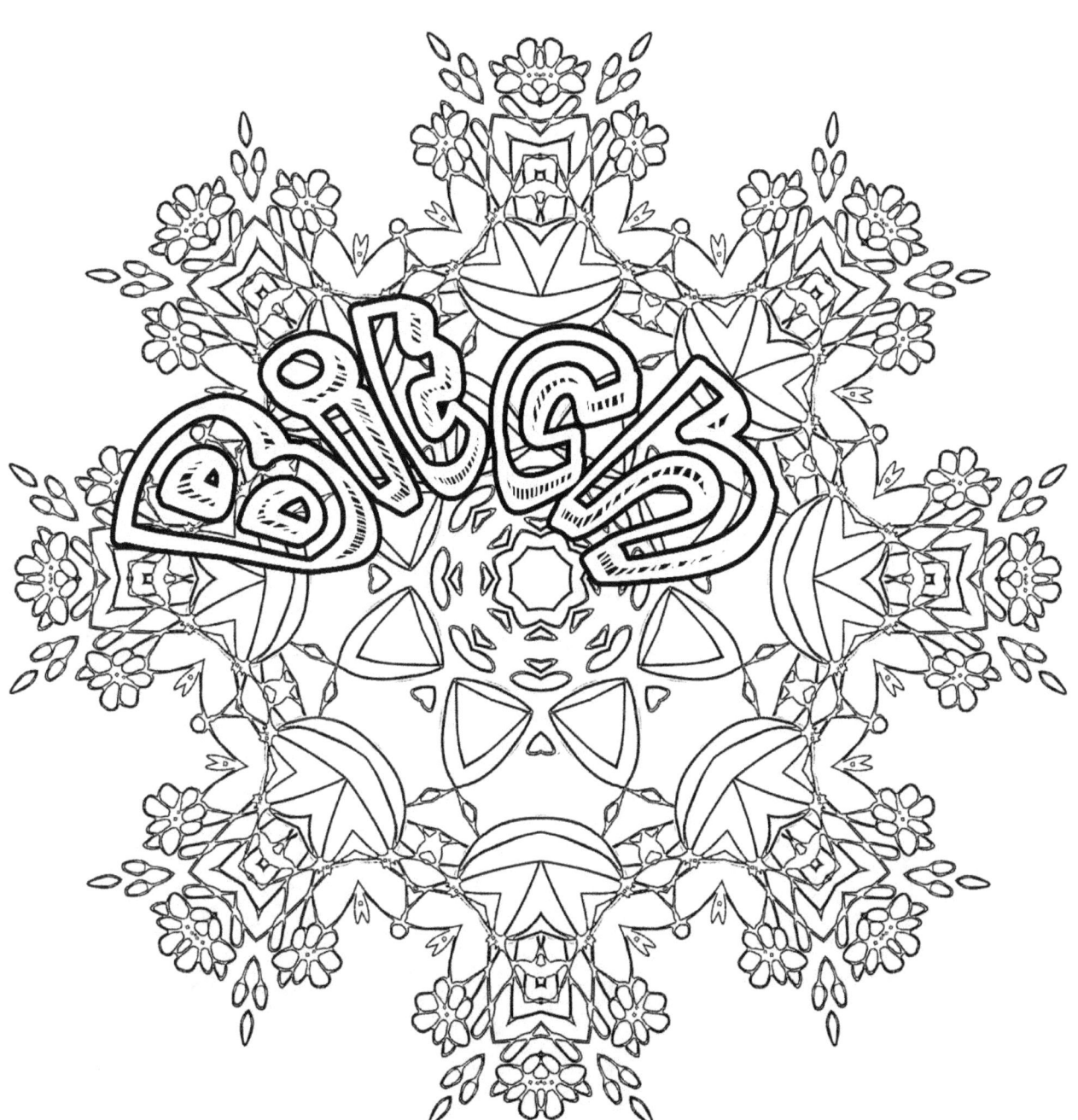

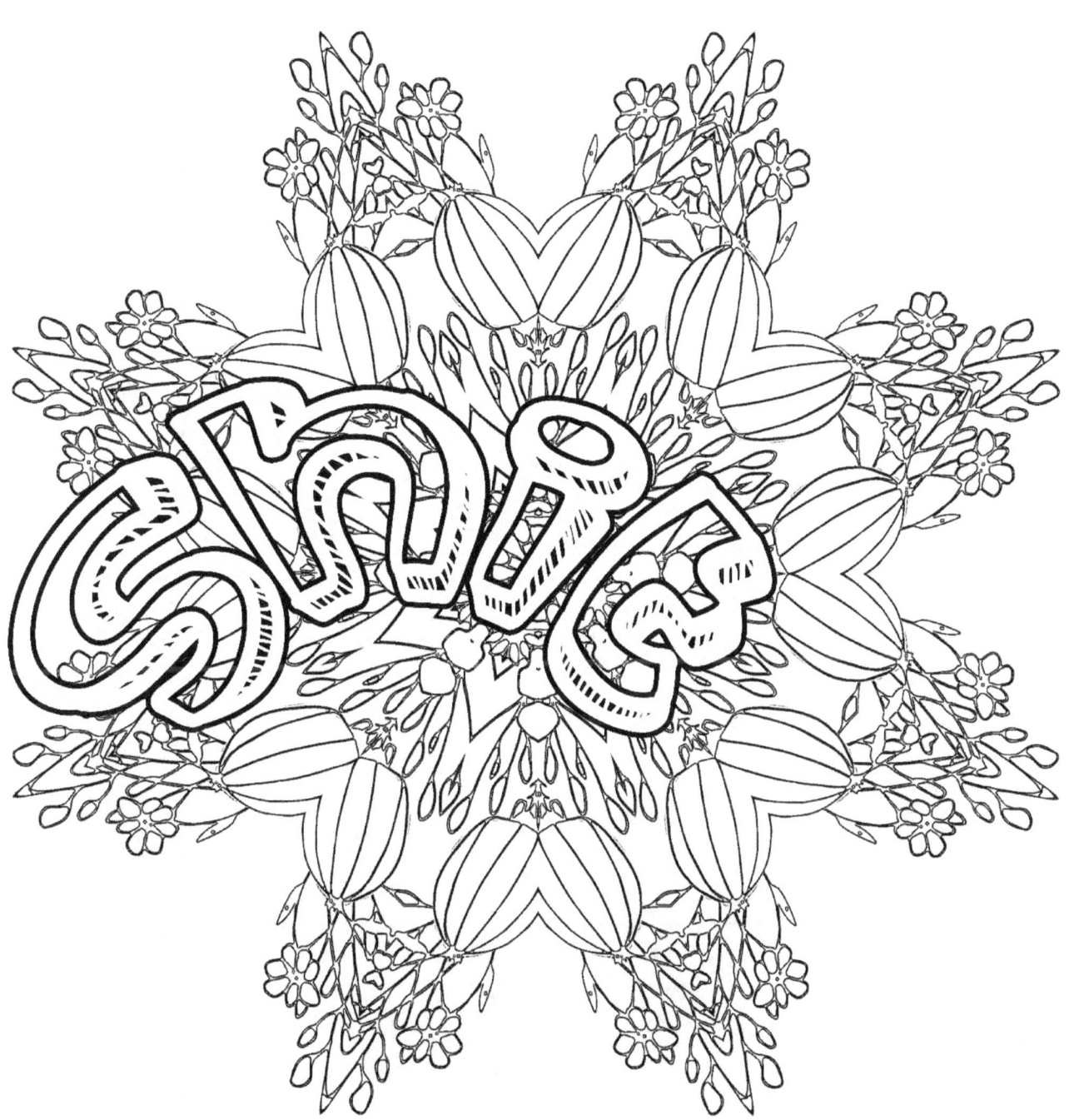

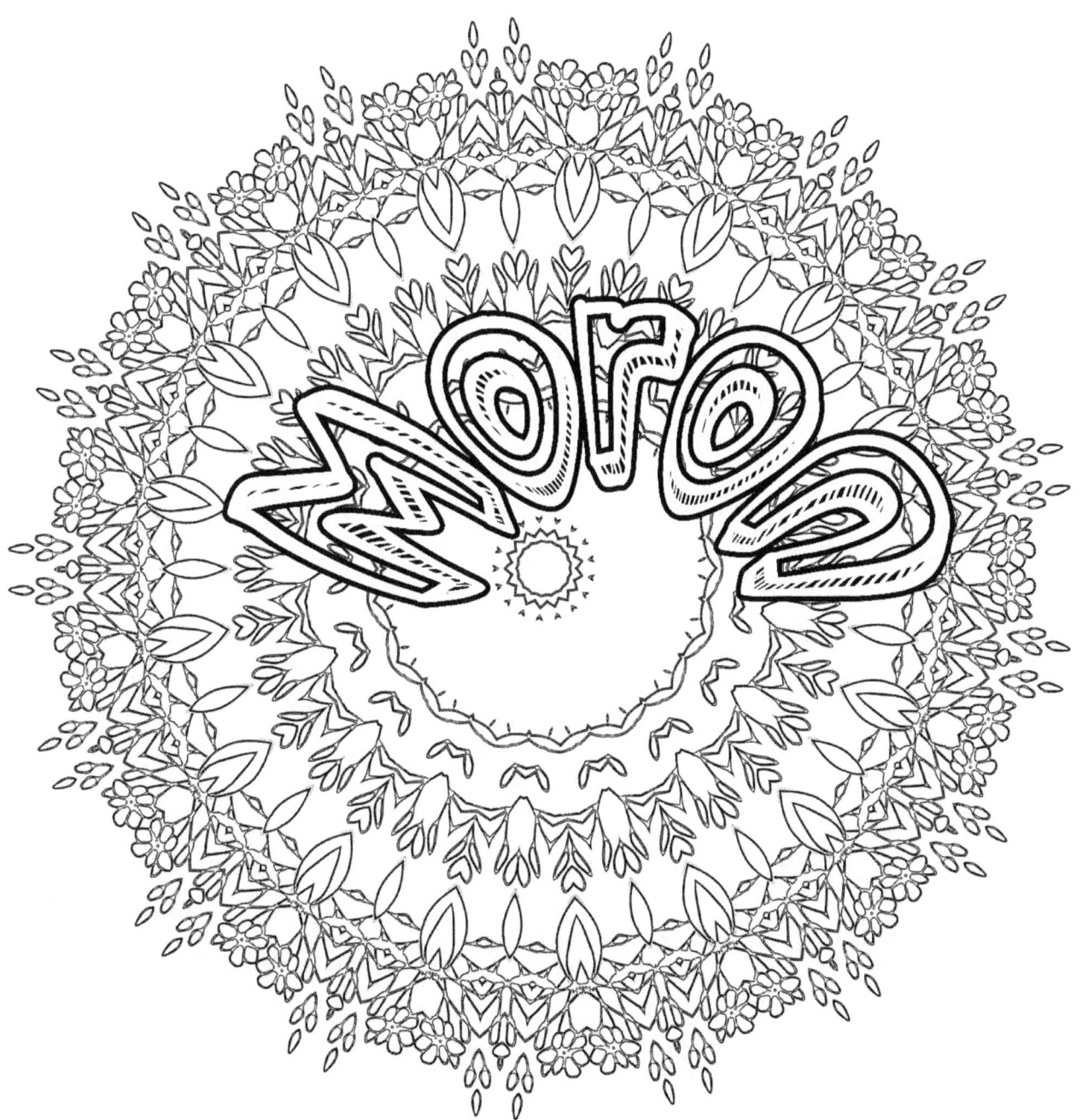

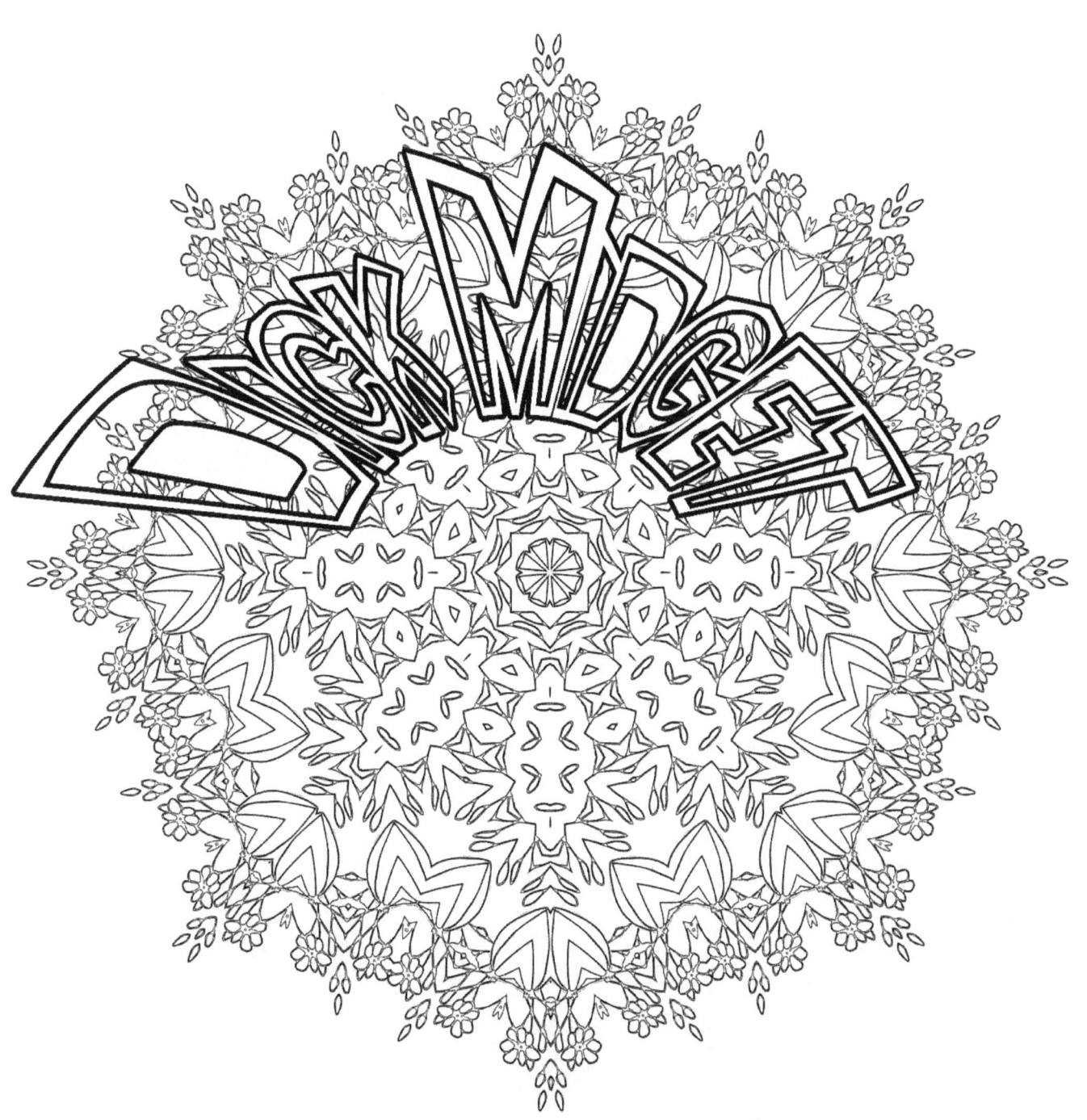

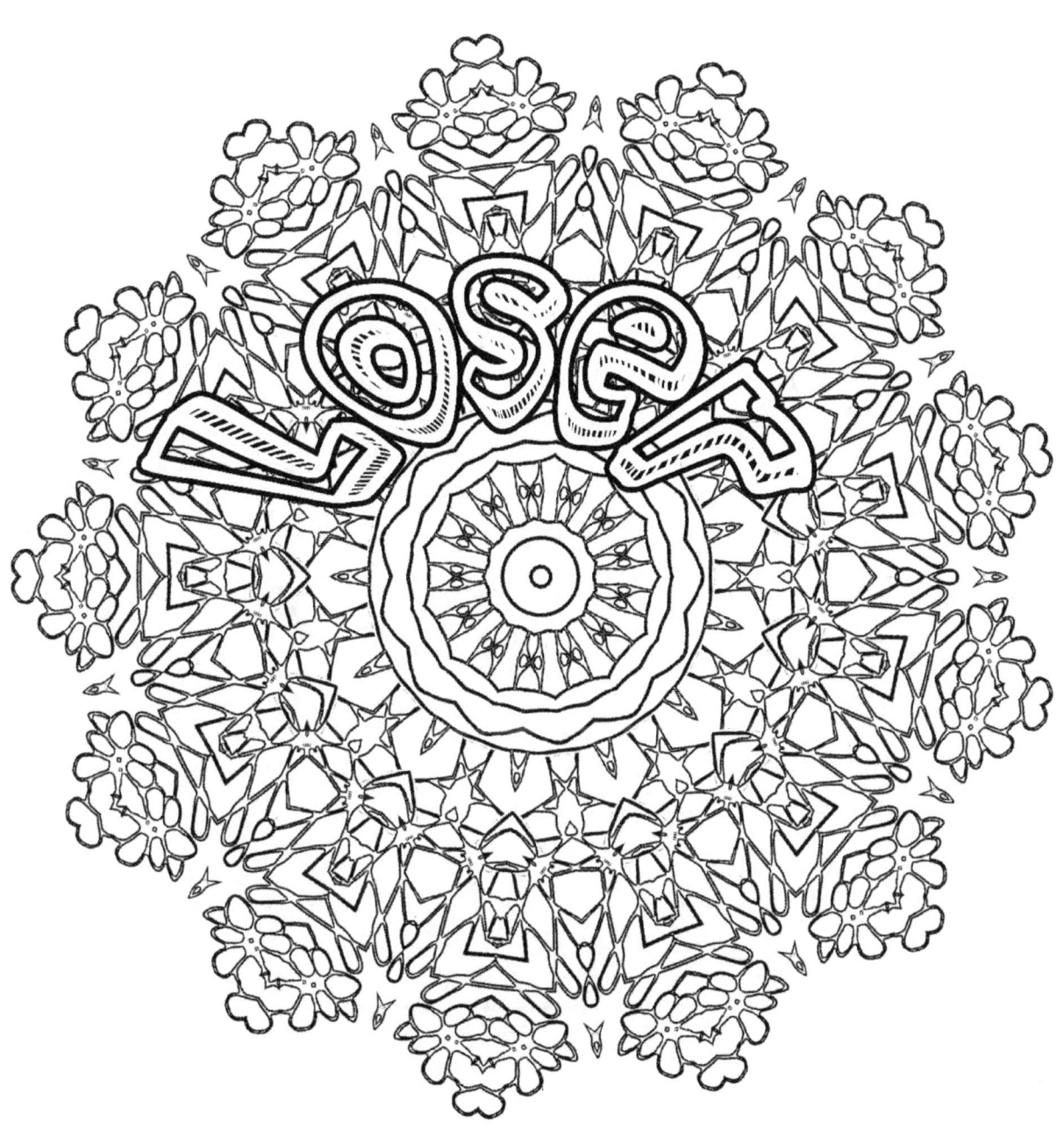

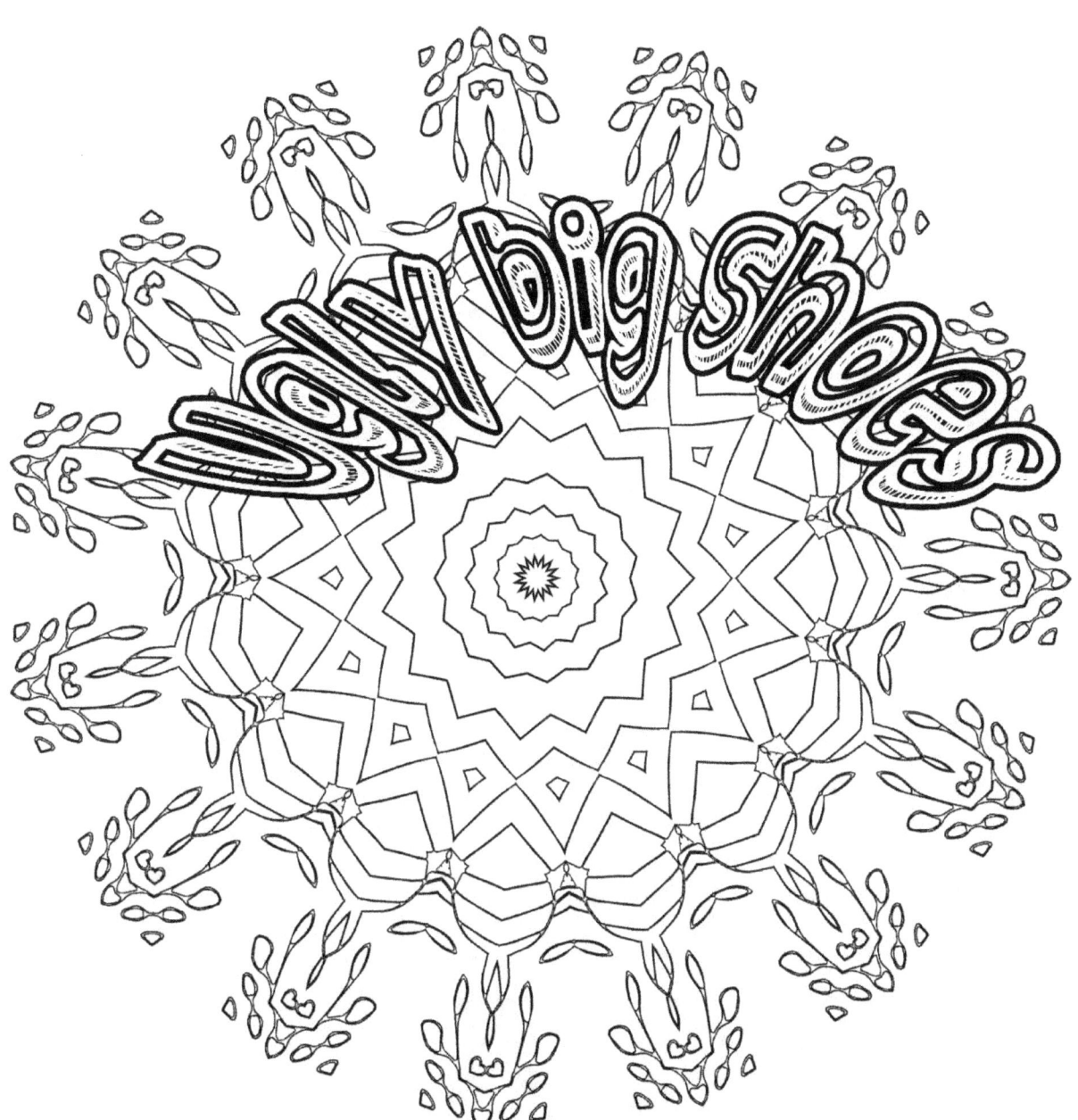

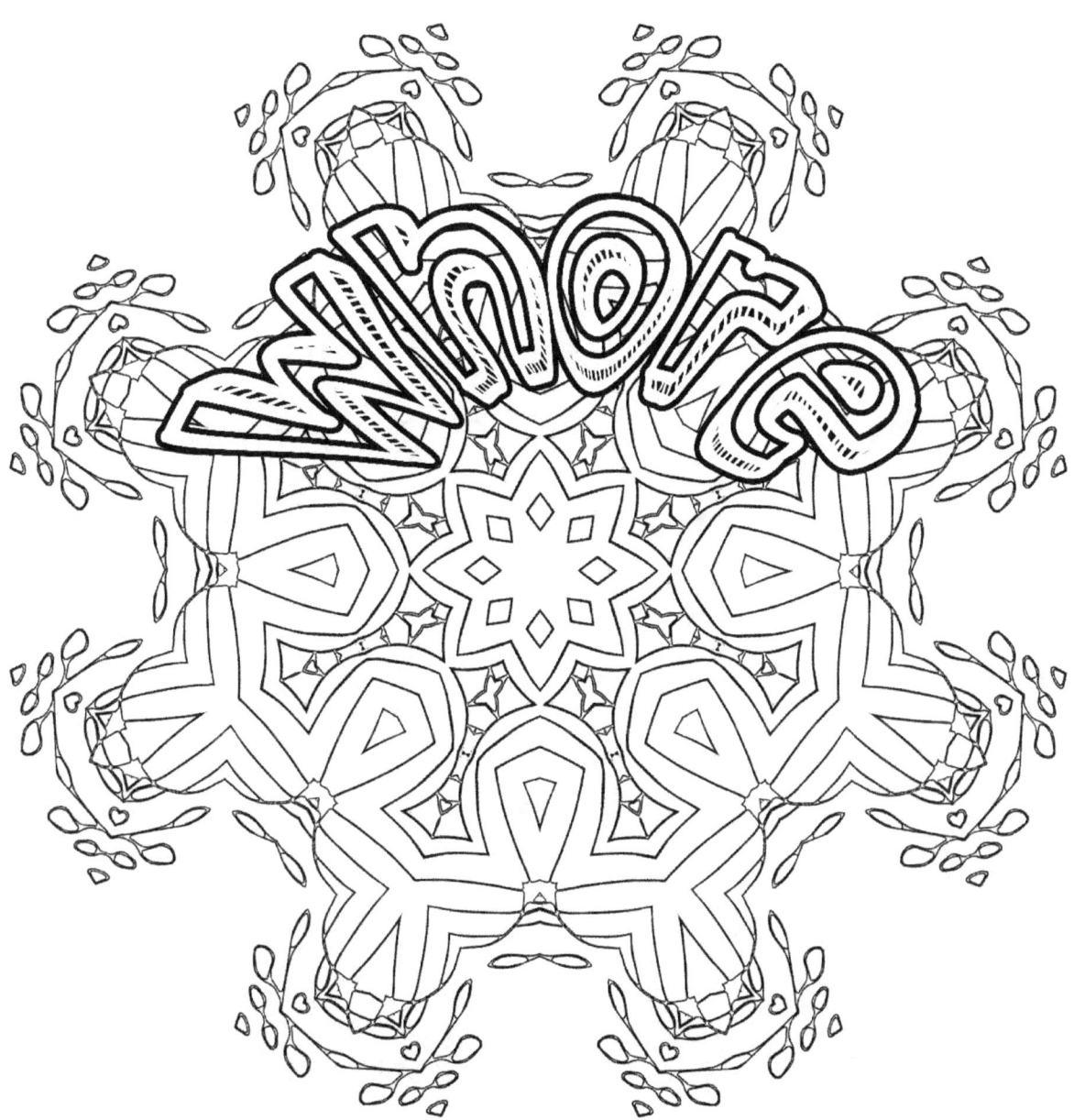

www.ingramcontent.com/pod-product-compliance
Lightning Source LLC
Chambersburg PA
CBHW081750170526
45167CB00009B/3985